WRITING MEDITATIONS

36 Prompts to Inspire Meditative Writing

By CM Hamilton

"Writing is its own reward."
--Henry Miller

CM HAMILTON
WRITING MEDITATIONS: 36 Prompts to Inspire Meditative Writing

© 2018 London

ISBN: 9781729332665

British spelling used throughout.
Book excerpt: http://bit.ly/writingmed
More writing meditations: http://bit.ly/writingmed5

Cover: Clay Collier
Interior photographs: Sergey Zolkin, Tom van Hoogstraten, Axel Antas-Bergkvist, Simson Petrol, Pietro De Grandi, Susan Yin

ALSO BY THE AUTHOR:

Meditations: 50 Meditation Techniques © 2018
For an extract of the book with instructions for six
fundamental meditation techniques, visit
https://bit.ly/50med.

- - -

Meditations for Sleep © 2019
For an extract of the book with instructions for four
sleeping meditations, visit https://bit.ly/sleepmed.

- - -

WRITING MEDITATIONS

36 Prompts to Inspire Meditative Writing

"Writing Meditations is a helpful catalogue of prompts to generate creativity and effective thinking." *MF*

"Daily exercises for daily improvement. Excellent." *QG*

Table of Contents

- - -

Quotes from the book

"Writing is its own reward."
--Henry Miller

"Get it down. Take chances. It may be bad, but it's the only way you can do anything really good."
--William Faulkner

"I write to discover what I know."
--Flannery O'Connor

"Ideas are like rabbits. You get a couple and learn how to handle them, and pretty soon you have a dozen."
--John Steinbeck

"If my doctor told me I had only six minutes to live, I wouldn't brood. I'd type a little faster."
--Isaac Asimov

Introduction

Writing meditations are short, 5- to 20-minute focused writing sessions that encourage creativity through mindful, diligent concentration. Writing meditations are an effective form of meditation and deliberate practice to reflect on important matters and improve decision making. Research has shown that writing exercises can have significant health benefits and increase productivity.

Many of history's greatest minds spent many hours writing things that were never meant to be seen by anyone. Scientists like Isaac Newton and Charles Darwin, politicians like Benjamin Franklin and Winston Churchill, artists like Leonardo Da Vinci and Ernest Hemingway, and historical figures like Marcus Aurelius and Abraham Lincoln all spent considerable time writing to no one but themselves. They understood that the deliberate practice of writing had significant benefits to their creativity, self-awareness, memory, productivity and well-being.

Regular focused writing can help you learn to process and communicate complex ideas effectively, memorise important information and brainstorm new ideas. Writing about your experiences and aspirations helps you see opportunities and organize concepts, as well as to help distil thoughts into to-do lists and specific actions. Writing can also provide a release valve for the stresses of your daily life and give you more control over your emotions and happiness.

Researchers have noted that deliberate writing sessions of as little as 15–20 minutes on 3–5 occasions were enough to help people deal with traumatic, stressful and emotional events. It is even effective for people with severe illnesses or who are experiencing sudden life changes and can work more effectively than other treatments.

You too can experience all the benefits of writing meditations, plus it is enjoyable, enlightening and easy to incorporate into your life as a daily habit.

- - -

Basics of Writing Meditation

How to use writing meditations, in a few words:

Select a "meditation" or writing prompt. Find a place where you are unlikely to be disturbed. Sit in a comfortable position and set a timer for 5–20 minutes. Spend up to a minute settling and preparing, then take a few deep breaths and begin to write.

To get the best results from writing meditations and journaling:

- Don't worry about grammar or spelling, just get thoughts into words on a page;

- Be open, honest and authentic with the knowledge that no one else is going to read it;

- Write by hand in cursive or short-hand if possible, although typing fast into a word processor can work as well (if you avoid editing);

- Write a lot – as much as you can in the available time.

Since writing meditations combine action with reflection, it can lead to more creativity and better decisions through increased awareness. There will be short and long term benefits.

This book provides simple and clear instructions for 36 different writing prompts to inspire meditative writing including: stream of consciousness writing, journaling, lists, poetry, mind maps, creative writing, affirmations, elevator pitches and deliberate planning techniques. The writing meditations are divided into three categories: Creative Thinking, Reflect/Decide, and Plans/Getting Things Done. At the end of the book there are 15 tips for more effective writing meditations.

Each writing meditation technique includes a full set of instructions. You don't need to read the book in chronological order, nor try all of the writing meditations. Flip through and find some that appeal to you. Try them out in one or a few sittings.

- - -

Types of Writing Meditation Prompts

There are many different meditation techniques and ways to classify them. For the purposes of this book, I have divided the writing meditations into three types:

- <u>Creative Thinking</u> – exercise your mind, make lists and be creative. There are 16 creative thinking techniques included in the first section of the book.

- <u>Reflect and Decide</u> – use the process of writing to reflect, improve and make better decisions. There are 10 reflective techniques included in the second section of the book.

- <u>Plans and Getting Things Done</u> – create deliberate plans for the future and write out the steps required to get things done. There are 10 planning techniques included in the third section of the book.

After these three main sections, there are 15 tips on how to use writing meditations, as well as some suggestions for very short writing meditations when you only have a few minutes to spare.

If you find the techniques and tips in this book useful, visit http://bit.ly/writingmed5 for five more writing meditations which are not included in the book.

Let's get started with the techniques.

Section I
Creative Thinking

Creative Thinking Writing Meditations – exercise your mind, make lists and be creative

"Get it down. Take chances. It may be bad, but it's the only way you can do anything really good."
--William Faulkner

10 Bad Ideas

Type: Creative Thinking
Summary: Write a list of 10 (or more) ideas about a new topic every day
Time: 5–15 minutes

This is a great exercise for creativity and exercising the mind, and for turning thoughts into actions. Set a timer for 5–15 minutes. At the top of the page write "10 bad ideas for [x]"; then proceed to write a list of at least ten ideas about today's topic.

The reason to title it "bad ideas" is that you don't want to labour over each idea and whether it is good or not. They are supposed to be bad ideas, so they can be unformed or badly formed. Change the list every day. Amongst the bad ideas there are often some incredibly good ideas.

For instance, the 10 bad ideas could be about:

- how to show more gratitude
- book titles or chapter names for an unwritten story
- a to-do list of next steps to complete a major project you are working on
- career changes you could make
- simple physical exercises you could do today
- gift ideas for an upcoming event or holiday
- healthy breakfast foods
- small things you could do that could make a positive impact this week
- ways to respond to a difficult person

- who and how could you help in a small way today
- a few ideas of how you could spend your time better or more meaningfully.

Lists often lead to new lists. For example, one day might be a list of 10 projects you want to work on. The next day will be 10 ideas for how to start one of those projects. The next day will be 10 ideas for people you could ask to help with this project. The next day will be 10 ideas of things you could accomplish today related to that project, etc, etc.

Your mind will wander, and when you realise that you are thinking about anything other than your list of bad ideas, return your focus to the writing meditation. Continue until the timer goes off.

- - -

Stream of Consciousness (Morning Pages)

Type: Creative Thinking
Summary: Start writing and don't stop, writing whatever comes to mind
Time: 5–20 minutes

Set a timer for 5–20 minutes and write for the full time, keeping the pen on the page and writing any thoughts that come to mind, whether they are lists, things to do, emotions, feelings, thoughts, goals, or dreams you recall.

One form of stream of consciousness writing popularised by Julia Cameron is called "morning pages," which she describes as *"three pages of longhand, stream of consciousness writing, done first thing in the morning."* She continues, *"There is no wrong way to do Morning Pages – they are not high art. They are not even 'writing.' They are about anything and everything that crosses your mind – and they are for your eyes only. Morning Pages provoke, clarify, comfort, cajole, prioritise and synchronise the day at hand. Do not over-think Morning Pages: just put three pages of anything on the page...and then do three more pages tomorrow."*

You'll be surprised to find things out about yourself that you didn't previously know or understand, and will discover that you can clarify your own thinking with this kind of stream of consciousness writing.

A fun stream of consciousness tool is the Most Dangerous Writing App. With this web based word processor you set a time (say five minutes) and if at any point during that time period you stop writing for more than five seconds everything gets deleted! If you make it to your full time without stopping you can save your work. You can find it at:

https://www.themostdangerouswritingapp.com/

Your mind will wander, but just keep writing down those wandering thoughts as fast as you can. Don't stop. Continue until the timer goes off.

- - -

Time Capsule

Type: Creative Thinking
Summary: Create a written time capsule about your life right now
Time: 10–20 minutes

This meditation is fun, and it is an excellent way to increase awareness of how your mind works and how you might be happier, less worried or more motivated to do important and meaningful things.

Set a timer for 10–20 minutes. At the top of the page write "Time Capsule [Date]", and then proceed to create a written time capsule of your life right now (or this month).

Write a long list or many paragraphs about your life right now, including:

- people who are important in your day-to-day life
- something recently bought
- thoughts about your current financial situation
- things you are currently worried about
- short term goals
- music, books, media and entertainment that you are enjoying
- how you spend your days
- important events in the news (and/or headlines in the news)
- written descriptions of some photographs you've recently taken
- trips, vacations and recent holidays

- details of a recent visit to/with family
- details of your home, bedroom and living situation
- a meal or restaurant you have recently enjoyed
- thoughts about your job, career and work colleagues.

Use these suggestions above as a questionnaire or write in any form about your present situation. When you've finished, photograph, scan or save this time capsule into a google calendar or other software where you can select a date in the future to read it. At some point in the future, maybe in 2 or 6 or 12 months' time, read it. The experience will probably lead to interesting insights about how you worry, how you change (or not) in the short term, how important things become unimportant and vice versa.

Your mind will wander, and when you realise that you are thinking about anything other than the written time capsule, return your focus to the writing meditation. Continue until the timer goes off.

- - -

Life as a Three-Act Play

Type: Creative Thinking
Summary: Write about your life or current year in the form of a three-act play
Time: 10–20 minutes

Set a timer for 10–20 minutes. At the top of the page write "My Life as a Three-Act Play", then "Fade In". Proceed to write an outline in three acts, using yourself as the main character and your life (or this year) as the story with some goals, setbacks, and a few fictional elements.

This exercise can be used to explore a big decision, a relationship, an adventure or upcoming move, including what obstacles you might encounter and how characters react. Use a three-act structure template that you are familiar with, or you can find many examples online. See one example in the diagram on the next page.

Typically, the first act will establish the main characters, their relationships and the world they live in. A dynamic incident occurs that confronts the main character, whose attempts to deal with this incident lead to a second and more dramatic situation (known as the first turning point). Life will never be the same again for the protagonist, which raises a dramatic question.

In the second act, "rising action" depicts the protagonist's attempt to resolve the problem initiated by the first turning point, only to find they are in ever worsening situations. The protagonist must learn new skills and arrive at a higher sense of awareness of who they are and what they are capable of in order to deal with their predicament and with the help of other characters.

The third act features the resolution of the story and includes a climax where the main tensions of the story are brought to their most intense point and the dramatic question is answered. The protagonist and other characters are left with a new sense of who they really are.

Your mind will wander, and when you realise that you are thinking about anything other than your personal three-act story, return your focus to the writing meditation. Continue until the timer goes off.

Three-Act Diagram

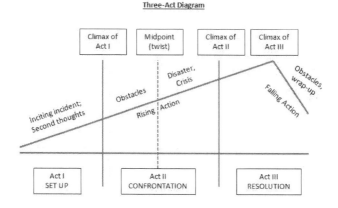

- - -

Letter to a Hero

Type: Creative Thinking
Summary: Write a letter to a hero of yours to tell them how they've inspired you
Time: 10–20 minutes

Set a timer for 10–20 minutes. At the top of the page write "Letter to [Hero]", and insert the name of anyone alive or dead whom you admire. Write them a letter about how they have inspired you and how you strive to be more like them.

This writing meditation can be effective for using a hero as a hypothetical accountability partner or to reflect on how you can be more like those who you admire. Simply write a letter addressed to this hero where you express gratitude for the ways in which they have inspired you and also describe the ways in which you are on the path to being more like them or are working on projects that relate directly to that inspiration.

This writing meditation also works well as a daily or regular journal entry, where instead of "Dear diary/journal" you would address it to a hero.

Your mind will wander, and when you realise that you are thinking about anything other than the letter to a hero, return your focus to the writing meditation. Continue until the timer goes off.

- - -

One Month to Live

Type: Creative Thinking
Summary: Write a list or plan of things to do if you had one month to live
Time: 10–20 minutes

This is a great exercise for focusing on important things and bringing more meaning to your day-to-day life.

Set a timer for 10–20 minutes. At the top of the page write "One Month to Live", and then proceed to write a list or summary of all the things you want or need to do with only one month left to live.

The format is not important – it can be a list, prose, stream of consciousness or just a collection of written thoughts. What do you need or want to get done in these final thirty days of life? How do you go about arranging your time and what steps do you take to get those things done? Think of different areas of your life: family, people, unresolved conflicts, finances, bucket list items. How can you make your life and these thirty days of remaining time on earth as meaningful as possible?

This writing meditation also works well as a month-long journaling exercise. Once you have the list of things to do if you only had one month to live, try to do some or many of those things over a thirty-day period and keep track of daily progress during the month.

Your mind will wander, and when you realise that you are thinking about anything other than the most important things to do during your last month, return your focus to the writing meditation. Continue until the timer goes off.

- - -

Gratitude List/Journal

Type: Creative Thinking
Summary: Journal or write a long list of things you are grateful for
Time: 5–20 minutes

Many people and experts agree that one way to be happier is to focus on gratitude and be more aware of the things you are grateful for.

Set a timer for 5–20 minutes. At the top of the page write "Gratitude", and then proceed to write a list, journal or summary of all the things you are grateful for.

Reflect on all things great and small for which you have gratitude, both directly and indirectly. These could be your health, family and friends, ancestors, community, music, knowledge and the things that bring you joy. They could be challenges, emotions, goals achieved and not, your immediate surroundings and comforts, fresh air and rain, refrigeration, electricity or the ability to read. There are literally thousands and thousands of things to be grateful for. It may seem difficult at first, but it gets easier with continuous practice. Just keep going and write more and more things that you are grateful for.

Your mind will wander, and when you realise that you are thinking about anything other than adding more things you are grateful for, return your focus to the writing meditation. Continue until the timer goes off.

Character Sketch

Type: Creative Thinking
Summary: Write about yourself or someone else using a fictional character sketch template
Time: 10–20 minutes

Set a timer for 10–20 minutes. At the top of the page write "Character Sketch – [Name]", adding your name or the name of someone else in your life. Proceed to write a character sketch including physical details, personality traits, motivations, flaws and relevance in the 'story'.

This exercise can be an interesting way to explore people in your life and their 'role' in your life, including attributes, detriments and potential conflicts.

Use any one-page character sketch template that you are familiar with, or you can find many examples online. One format is to divide a page into box diagrams with headings such as: Relevance to Story, Connections to Other Characters, Dominant Character Trait or Emotion, Physical Description, Relevant Background, Minor Flaws, Key Flaw, Redeeming Qualities, Enemies or Conflicts, and Driving Motivation. See diagram on the next page.

Your mind will wander, and when you realise that you are thinking about anything other than the character sketch, return your focus to the writing meditation. Continue until the timer goes off.

Character Sketch

Story:
Character:
Relevance to Story:

Driving Motivation:

Dominant Character Trait

Physical Description:

Redeeming Qualities:

Connection to other Characters:

Key Flaw:

Enemies or Conflicts:

Relevant Background:

Minor Flaws:

- - -

Constructive Feedback

Type: Creative Thinking
Summary: Reflect on your performance at a recent task or event and write ways you could improve for next time
Time: 10–20 minutes

Set a timer for 10–20 minutes. At the top of the page write "Constructive Feedback", and then proceed to write a list or summary to yourself about the ways in which you could improve at a job, task or how you could have done better in a recent performance.

Think about any important task you have completed recently, perhaps a job interview or discussion with a loved one, an exam, meeting, performance, holiday, event, etc. Write yourself constructive feedback about how you could have done better, what you would have changed, and what steps you can take to improve for the next time. Reflect on your actual performance, and be aware of where you could improve and how.

This writing meditation also works well as an end-of-the-day journal entry. Simply write ways that you could have improved the day, or how you could have taken ownership or control of your happiness, achievements, emotions, tasks, or other aspects of your life today.

Your mind will wander, and when you realise that you are thinking about anything other than the constructive feedback, return your focus to the writing meditation. Continue until the timer goes off.

Proust Questionnaire

Type: Creative Thinking
Summary: Write answers to some of life's great questions from the Proust Questionnaire
Time: 20 minutes

Set a timer for 20 minutes. At the top of the page write "Proust Questionnaire", and then proceed to write answers to some of the questions from the Proust Questionnaire. It may take more than one sitting to answer all of them.

A 35-question parlour game was popularized (though not devised) by the French essayist and novelist Marcel Proust, who believed that an individual reveals his or her true nature in answering the questions. Vanity Fair magazine regularly published answers to these questions provided by the celebrities that they interviewed for magazine article profiles. Write responses to some or all of these fifteen prompts from the Proust Questionnaire:

1. What is your idea of perfect happiness?

2. What is your greatest fear?

3. What is the trait you most deplore in yourself?

4. What is the trait you most deplore in others?

5. Which living person do you most admire?

6. What is your greatest extravagance?

7. What is your current state of mind?

8. When and where were you happiest?

9. Which talent would you most like to have?

10. If you could change one thing about yourself, what would it be?

11. What do you consider your greatest achievement?

12. Where would you most like to live?

13. Which historical figure do you most identify with?

14. How would you like to die?

15. What is your motto?

Your mind will wander, and when you realise that you are thinking about anything other than the Proust Questionnaire, return your focus to the writing meditation. Continue until the timer goes off. It may take more than one sitting to complete.

- - -

Haiku

Type: Creative Thinking
Summary: Write a few haiku
Time: 10–20 minutes

Set a timer for 10–20 minutes. At the top of the page write "Haiku", and then proceed to write three, five or ten haiku.

Haiku is a very short traditional Japanese poem with 3 lines and 17 syllables. The first line should have 5 syllables, the second line 7 syllables, and the third line, again, 5 syllables. This simple 5-7-5 structure uses an economy of words to express profound and layered messages. The short length and specific structure lends itself to the focused attention of meditation and can create a mindful, diligent concentration.

Haiku can be deep and profound, but they can also be simple, mundane or silly. Here are a few examples of haiku that conform to the 5-7-5 structure:

Senator Dodd saw
his proposal melt like ice
in the noonday sun. (from NY Times Haiku)

On Friday evenings,
Men sit in the back swapping
Fish tales in Polish. (from NY Times Haiku)

There is power in
Knowledge, but there is greater
power in Wisdom (Neil deGrasse Tyson on Twitter)

Netflix and pizza
Please do not disturb me, guys
I am so busy (from Cosmopolitan magazine)

Your mind will wander, and when you realise that you are thinking about anything other than the haiku, return your focus to the writing meditation. Continue until the timer goes off.

- - -

Tribe of Mentors Questionnaire

Type: Creative Thinking
Summary: Write answers to the 11 questions in Tim Ferriss' Tribe of Mentors Questionnaire
Time: 20 minutes

Set a timer for 20 minutes. At the top of the page write "Tribe of Mentors Questionnaire", and then proceed to write answers to the 11 questions in Tim Ferriss' Tribe of Mentors Questionnaire.

As Tim Ferriss, the author, podcaster, interviewer, marketer, seeker and lost-soul approached the age of forty he came up with a list of questions to ask the 100+ people he most respected. He published the results in his book "Tribe of Mentors" in 2018. The questionnaire is as follows:

1. What is the book you've given most as a gift, and why? Or what are one to three books that have greatly influenced your life?
2. What purchase of less than $100 (£100 or €100) has most positively impacted your life in the last six months (or in recent memory)?
3. How has a failure, or apparent failure, set you up for later success? Do you have a "favorite failure"?
4. If you could have a gigantic billboard anywhere with anything on it – metaphorically speaking, getting a message out to millions or billions – what would it say and why? It could be a few

words or a paragraph. (If helpful, it can be someone else's quote: Are there any quotes you think of often or live your life by?)

5. What is one of the best or most worthwhile investments you've ever made? (It could be an investment of money, time, energy, etc.)

6. What is an unusual habit or an absurd thing that you love?

7. In the last five years, what new belief, behavior, or habit has most improved your life?

8. What advice would you give to a smart, driven college student about to enter the "real world"? What advice should they ignore?

9. What are bad recommendations you hear in your profession or area of expertise?

10. In the last five years, what have you become better at saying "no" to (distractions, invitations, etc.)? What new realizations and/or approaches helped? Any other tips?

11. When you feel overwhelmed or unfocused, or have lost your focus temporarily, what do you do? (If helpful: What questions do you ask yourself?) What is your idea of perfect happiness?

Your mind will wander, and when you realise that you are thinking about anything other than the Tribe of Mentors Questionnaire, return your focus to the writing meditation. Continue until the timer goes off. It may take more than one sitting to complete.

Limerick

Type: Creative Thinking
Summary: Write a few limericks
Time: 10–20 minutes

Set a timer for 10-20 minutes. At the top of the page write "Limericks", and then proceed to write two, three or five limericks.

A limerick is a poem, often humorous and sometimes crude, in five-lines with a strict rhyme scheme of AABBA, in which the first, second and fifth line rhyme while the third and fourth lines are shorter and share a different rhyme. This simple structure and short length lends itself to the focused attention of meditation and can create a mindful, diligent concentration.

Edward Lear was an early practitioner of limericks, and his self-illustrated "Book of Nonsense" from 1846 remains a benchmark. He preferred the term "nonsense" to "limerick," and wrote many funny examples, including the following:

There was an Old Man with a beard,
Who said, "It is just as I feared!
  Two Owls and a Hen,
  Four Larks and a Wren,
Have all built their nests in my beard!"

Other famous limerick writers include Lord Alfred Tennyson, Rudyard Kipling and Robert Louis Stevenson.

The limerick example below is of unknown origin:

The limerick packs laughs anatomical
Into space that is quite economical.
  But the good ones I've seen
  So seldom are clean
And the clean ones so seldom are comical.

Limericks are particularly suited to be about people, and a good starting point to write limericks about people in your own life would be, for example, "There once was a boss named [Andy]…" or "There once was a wife named [Holly]…" or "There once was an unreasonable landlord…"

Your mind will wander, and when you realise that you are thinking about anything other than the limerick, return your focus to the writing meditation. Continue until the timer goes off.

- - -

Purge

Type: Creative Thinking
Summary: Purge your mind of worries, fears and stresses by letting them spill onto a page
Time: 5–20 minutes

Set a timer for 5–20 minutes and use this exercise to purge your mind of worries, fears, stresses, emotions and feelings that are distracting you from more important things.

It is common to let thoughts of worry and concern dominate your mind, to repeat previous conversations or arguments, or even to rehearse future conversations and arguments. This is detrimental to your ability to concentrate on more important things. When you need to purge your mind of these untimely or unhelpful thoughts, take time to write them down. The process of putting these thoughts on a page should help to quiet your mind so that it can focus on more important tasks.

This form of stream of consciousness writing can take many forms – an unstructured stream of consciousness writing session, a draft email or letter to someone which you will not actually send, bullet points or a list, a journal entry or other formats will work as well.

Your mind will wander, but just keep writing down those thoughts and concern in an effort to purge them from your mind. Continue until the timer goes off.

- - -

Letter to a Politician

Type: Creative Thinking
Summary: Write a letter to a politician
Time: 10–20 minutes

Set a timer for 10–20 minutes. At the top of the page write "Letter to [Politician]", which could be any politician at the local or national level. Write them a letter to thank them for their public service, and to make policy suggestions and discuss other ways of improving yours and their constituent's lives.

Many people have convictions and strong opinions about how to make their community, city or nation a better place. However, few people actually express these convictions in the form of written suggestions to their representative leaders. Use this writing meditation time to write a letter to a politician expressing your opinions and making credible suggestions for positive change. This can also be a good way to purge your mind of all of the things you see on social media and in the news that you feel helpless to change. Don't just express dissatisfaction – make concrete suggestions for change with good reasoning.

Your mind will wander, and when you realise that you are thinking about anything other than the letter to a politician, return your focus to the writing meditation. Continue until the timer goes off.

You might also follow through and actually send this letter.

Letter from a Space Ship

Type: Creative Thinking
Summary: Write a letter to family and friends as if you may never see them again
Time: 10–20 minutes

This is a great exercise for focusing on important things and bringing more meaning to your day-to-day life.

Set a timer for 10–20 minutes. At the top of the page write "Letter from a Space Ship", and write a letter to family and friends as if you may never see them again.

Imagine that you have been selected to tag along with astronauts on a trip to space, or that you and some fellow passengers are going to start a colony on the moon or Mars. On the launchpad after getting into the space ship and preparing for take-off you are told that there is a 20 minute delay, and you have just enough time to write one last letter to your family and friends or any one person in particular. Considering the enormity of the situation and the fact that you may never see them again, and with such a limited amount of time to say everything you need to say, write a concise letter in 20 minutes to say the important things.

Your mind will wander, and when you realise that you are thinking about anything other than the letter from a space ship, return your focus to the writing meditation. Continue until the timer goes off.

- - -

Section II
Reflect and Decide

Use the process of writing to reflect, improve and make better decisions.

"I write to discover what I know."
--Flannery O'Connor

Five People I Admire

Type: Reflect and Decide
Summary: Write down the attributes of five people you admire and how you might better exhibit those attributes
Time: 10–20 minutes

Set a timer for 10–20 minutes. At the top of the page write "Five People I Admire", and then proceed to write down attributes of those five people and how you might better exhibit their key attributes.

Think of five people who you admire – they may be significant figures from history, friends, acquaintances, members of your family, or well-known people in the public eye today. What are the key attributes of those people that you admire? Write a list or summarise the attributes which make them good and successful role models, as well as specific examples of how they exhibit those attributes. Examples might include honesty and integrity, good communication, empathy and service to others, creativity, success, work ethic, leadership qualities or many other attributes. What attributes or character traits have helped them achieve success?

By making a list of these admirable qualities and reflecting on attributes that you venerate, you should consider how you might exhibit these attributes in your daily life. Write some ideas of how you could develop these qualities or more regularly express them in your own life today and during the next week.

Your mind will wander, and when you realise that you are thinking about anything other than the list of admirable qualities, return your focus to the writing meditation. Continue until the timer goes off.

- - -

Decision Tree

Type: Reflect and Decide
Summary: Make a decision tree about an important decision
Time: 5–20 minutes

Set a timer for 5–20 minutes. At the top of the page write "Decision Tree - [Topic]", inserting the topic you are brainstorming or contemplating. Proceed to create a decision tree.

A decision tree visually arranges potential outcomes and possible consequences of a decision. It is a form of "second level thinking" used to consider the immediate and subsequent outcomes of a decision. Decision trees are commonly used in decision analysis to help identify a strategy most likely to reach a goal, and they are a popular tool in machine learning and for creating algorithms. They can be structured from left to right or top to bottom. You may have seen infographics on the internet (often humorous) which use this kind of structure.

A decision tree is a flowchart-like structure in which each branch represents a key outcome and follow-on consequences or actions. Start by writing the decision in one or a few words at the left or top of a page. Then write some possible outcomes of that decision, and consequences or subsequent impacts of those outcomes. See an example image below.

Decision trees allow you to organise the possible consequences of a decision in an objective way, and also help stimulate creativity and open your mind to other options that might be available. They are simple to understand and interpret, and important insights can be gleaned. It will help you determine worst, best or alternative options for different scenarios.

Your mind will wander, and when you realise that you are thinking about anything other than your decision tree, return your focus to the writing meditation. Continue until the timer goes off.

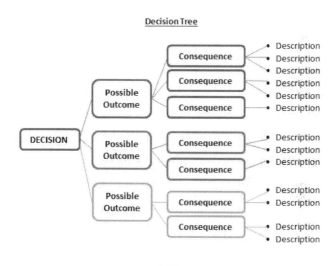

Decision Tree

- - -

How to Enjoy This Holiday

Type: Reflect and Decide
Summary: Brainstorm in advance and write a list of ways to improve and enjoy a holiday
Time: 10–20 minutes

Set a timer for 10–20 minutes. At the top of the page write "How to Enjoy This Holiday", and then proceed to write a list or summary of all ways that you can improve and better enjoy an upcoming holiday.

Whether travelling to a new location, seeing family for the holidays, or taking the kids camping, we all look forward to vacations with expectations of cheerfulness, excitement, relaxation and happiness. The reality can often be quite different. Humans routinely and unintentionally undermine holidays by letting small things get to us, falling into old patterns and routines, and not using time as wisely as we could.

In advance of a holiday, trip or visit with family, write a list of things you can do to enjoy the holiday. It can be fairly easy to write a long list of small things which you can do in advance, during travel and while away which will make a big difference to yours and others' experience of the holiday. Alternatively, or in addition to doing this exercise in advance of travel, you can do this on any morning of your holiday to prepare for the day ahead.

Your mind will wander, and when you realise that you are thinking about anything other than the ways that you can improve and enhance the holiday experience, return your focus to the writing meditation. Continue until the timer goes off.

- - -

Stoic Virtues

Type: Reflect and Decide
Summary: Write some ways in which you might better exhibit the four stoic virtues of Wisdom, Courage, Justice and Temperance
Time: 10–20 minutes

Set a timer for 10–20 minutes. At the top of the page write "Stoic Virtues", and then proceed to write ways in which you might better exhibit the four stoic virtues.

The Stoics thought that the good life (Eudaimonia or "flourishing") consisted in cultivating one's moral virtues in order to become a better person. The four cardinal virtues were: Wisdom (sophia), Courage (andreia), Justice (dikaiosyne), and Temperance (sophrosyne).

Consider these definitions:

Wisdom: knowledge through experience; an ability to exercise good judgement.

Courage: the ability to do something despite fear; strength in the face of pain or grief.

Justice: being fair and reasonable to others.

Temperance: excellence of character by exhibiting moderation and self-control.

How could you gain wisdom though experience or exercise good judgement this week? What hurdle or challenge will require courage this week? To whom can you be just towards and in what way? How exactly can you exhibit moderation and self-control in the coming days? Write a list or thoughts about how you can exhibit these specific qualities today and this week.

Your mind will wander, and when you realise that you are thinking about anything other than the ways in which you can better exhibit the four stoic virtues, return your focus to the writing meditation. Continue until the timer goes off.

- - -

Less More None

Type: Reflect and Decide
Summary: Write a list of activities you want to do less often, more often, and not at all
Time: 10–20 minutes

Set a timer for 10–20 minutes. At the top of the page write "Less More None", and then proceed to write a list of activities that you want to do less often, more often, and not at all.

Jacoby Young, who works at an elementary school in Hawaii, created a list called "Less More None", which details the activities he wants to do less often, more often, and not at all. From the list Jacoby published on his website he includes: less online shopping, more learning Hawaiian history, and no adding new debt. Other examples might include less social media, more time outside, and no working on holidays. Choose five, ten or more items for each category.

Jacoby's original post can be found at: https://www.jacobyyoung.com/lmn.

This is a great short, focused writing meditation to reflect on small but significant changes you can make in your daily life.

Your mind will wander, and when you realise that you are thinking about anything other than the Less More None list, return your focus to the writing meditation. Continue until the timer goes off.

Affirmations

Type: Reflect and Decide
Summary: Write a statement of affirmation twenty times
Time: 2–5 minutes

An affirmation is a deliberate, repeated written statement. It is a form of positive thinking and self-empowerment that can be an effective way of achieving or moving towards a goal. The statement should be in the present tense, positive, personal and specific.

At the top of the page write "Affirmation" or the topic of your affirmation, and then proceed to write a statement of affirmation twenty times. Repeat this exercise daily for a month or more. Craft your own affirmation, or take inspiration from these examples:

- I, (name), can (do something) and (achieve stated goal)

- Today there will be many challenges, but I am a problem solver

- I have control of my attitude and actions, and therefore of my happiness and unhappiness

- I take ownership of everything that happens, especially my attitude and reactions

- Problems are puzzles that are fun to solve

- Fearlessness is not the absence of fear; it is confronting the fear and doing it anyway

- Today I will do something different which is slightly outside of my comfort zone

- The impediment to action advances action

- The obstacle is the way

An affirmation should not be a lie, inaccurate or insincere. For example, "I am king of the world" is a lie and disingenuous. Instead, create an affirmation which is positive and accurate, oriented towards your goals, and something that you can control without being untrue. A quick search for affirmations on the internet will provide many more examples.

Your mind will wander, and if you realise that you are thinking about anything other than the affirmation, return your focus to the writing meditation. Write it twenty times.

- - -

Pros and Cons

Type: Reflect and Decide
Summary: Make a list of pros and cons to help make a decision
Time: 5–20 minutes

Set a timer for 5–20 minutes. At the top of the page write "Pros and Cons for [Decision]", inserting whatever decision you are contemplating. Proceed to write a long list of pros and cons.

Write a list of advantages and disadvantages of a particular action, decision or goal. First, just write every pro and con you can think of. Keep adding to each list as the ideas come, or focus entirely on one list, then the other. Also add any follow-on consequences or different perspectives on the same item, or why the same thing might be a pro and a con.

Reflect on the list to make the decision, but don't fool yourself into thinking that the side with the bigger list wins. Consider how strong the arguments are and whether you might be repeating the same thing or comparing weak arguments to strong arguments. For instance, a long list of pros might be outweighed by one important con. Another common issue with pro and con lists is ignoring follow-on consequences of a decision. This will require 'second order thinking', which is considering next steps, potential consequences, and new problems that can arise from solving original problems. As long as you know these drawbacks going in, you can reflect appropriately on the pro/con list.

Your mind will wander, and when you realise that you are thinking about anything other than your list of pros and cons, return your focus to the writing meditation. Continue until the timer goes off.

- - -

Worst-Case Scenario

Type: Reflect and Decide
Summary: For an upcoming event, list some things that could go wrong and how you could respond in each case
Time: 5–20 minutes

Set a timer for 5–20 minutes. At the top of the page write "Worst-Case Scenario", and for an upcoming event or situation list one or more things that could go wrong, as well as some ideas about how you could respond in each case.

Worrying about an upcoming event or activity can be very counter-productive, but writing about it with some possible solutions will be constructive and help to set your mind at ease. First write the worst-case scenario – the thing that could go wrong, or all of the things that could go wrong. Don't hold back. Make it terrible.

After you have described this worst-case scenario and the things that could go wrong, write or list some potential responses or reactions in each case. The solutions don't have to be perfect or even great ideas; just try to be creative and honest about what kind of constructive response you could have in these situations. Doing so you will open up your mind to options and prepare you to respond, which will cause you to worry less and to perform better on the day.

Your mind will wander, and when you realise that you are thinking about anything other than the possible problems and potential solutions, return your focus to the writing meditation. Continue until the timer goes off.

- - -

Mind Map

Type: Reflect and Decide
Summary: Make a mind map for brainstorming or to help make a decision
Time: 5–20 minutes

Set a timer for 5–20 minutes. At the top of the page write "Mind Map - [Topic]", inserting the topic you are brainstorming or contemplating. Proceed to create a mind map.

A mind map is a way of visually arranging words and thoughts used as a form of brainstorming to structure, organise and consider information. It presents an overview that fuses words and ideas, which blends logic and creativity to help you think more proficiently and effectively about a subject. Mind maps can help you become more creative, remember more and solve problems more effectively. It is a diagram that connects information around a central subject, like a wheel with spokes which branch out into many sections. See an example mind map diagram on the next page.

Start by writing the topic in one or a few words at the centre of a page. Then draw four to six lines or branches off this word with key ideas, concepts or attributes of the main topic. From those subheadings, keep branching out. Make connections between branches in different areas of the page. Drawing mind maps allows you to collect thoughts and ideas in an objective way, and also helps stimulate connections and creativity. A mind map can help you see the big picture while also allowing you to explore detailed snippets of information. It can help you reduce mental clutter and cope with information overload, and can accelerate your ability to solve complex problems with creative insights and ideas.

Your mind will wander, and when you realise that you are thinking about anything other than your mind map, return your focus to the writing meditation. Continue until the timer goes off.

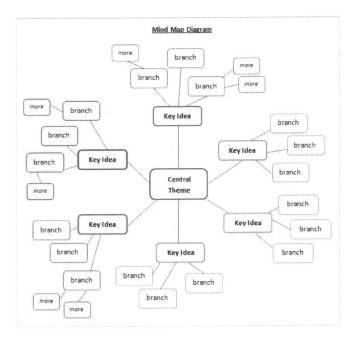

- - -

New Year's Resolutions

Type: Reflect and Decide
Summary: Write your New Year's (or New Month's) Resolutions
Time: 5–20 minutes

Set a timer for 5–20 minutes. At the top of the page write "New Year's Resolutions - [Year]", and then proceed to write those resolutions in an organised and structured way.

New Year's resolutions are regularly made and widely failed. The desire for positive change and difficulty in following through is part of the human condition. Instead of giving up, use this writing meditation to write good, structured resolutions that you are more likely to keep.

Some suggestions for creating a better list:

- Keep the list relatively short and focused on key resolutions;
- Be specific – include some concrete steps for starting and maintaining habits;
- Don't use repeats from previous years (or rewrite former resolutions in a better way);
- Forcing yourself to do unpleasant and inconvenient things won't work. Find a way to make the resolutions enjoyable and able to fit into your usual schedule.
- Refer back to the list often – affix it to a wardrobe door, mirror or other visible location.

You don't have to start your New Year's Resolutions on January 1st. Ancient Babylonians celebrated the beginning of a new year on what is now March 23rd. Late March and springtime is probably a more logical time to make changes in your life, although you can start (or re-start) your resolutions at any time. Some religions and cultures start each new year in February or September. In fact, the best time to write resolutions for the next twelve months is probably right now.

Another idea is New Month's Resolutions, where instead of committing for a whole year you just commit for one month. This is a great way to trial changes and to slowly build habits. You can do anything for one month.

Your mind will wander, and when you realise that you are thinking about anything other than writing your resolutions, return your focus to the writing meditation. Continue until the timer goes off.

- - -

Section III
Plans and Getting Things Done

Create deliberate plans for the future and write out the steps required to get things done.

"Ideas are like rabbits. You get a couple and learn how to handle them, and pretty soon you have a dozen."
— *John Steinbeck*

Things-to-do This Weekend

Type: Plans and Getting Things Done
Summary: Write a list of things to do this weekend
Time: 5–20 minutes

This sounds like a modest and unexciting exercise, but it can have a profound and positive impact on your life. The weekend goes too quickly and that dreaded Sunday evening depression is felt by many. A very common thought is: Where did the time go?

A simple to-do list, prepared in advance and referenced during the weekend, can act as a powerful tool to ensure we use our time more wisely and do not waste the weekend. It can help us to balance relaxation and chores, entertainment and activity.

Do this meditation on Friday or first thing Saturday morning. Set a timer for 5–20 minutes. At the top of the page write "Things-to-do This Weekend", and then proceed to write a detailed list.

Write down everything from chores and tasks, entertainment and fun, booking events and travels for the future, small steps you can make towards long term goals, communications with family and friends, financial and administrative tasks, cleaning, research, shopping, meals, things to read and educational opportunities, etc. Refer back often during the weekend, especially if you realise that you are wasting time or not using it wisely.

Using your time effectively on the weekend can have a significant impact on your life and levels of happiness.

Your mind will wander, and when you realise that you are thinking about anything other than the weekend list, return your focus to the writing meditation. Continue until the timer goes off.

- - -

Worry About It Later

Type: Plans and Getting Things Done
Summary: Write a list of things to worry about later, then set it aside and work on important things
Time: 2–10 minutes

Set a timer for 2–10 minutes. On a notecard or at the top of a page write "Worry About It Later", and then proceed to write all the things which you should or could worry about, but which are not urgent in the present moment.

Worrying and contemplating downside scenarios can be important and effective, but humans often spend too much time and mental capacity worrying about things unnecessarily. This persistent worry can divert attention from the present moment and more important things. One very effective way to deal with this is to make a Worry About It Later list. Spend a short, focused period of time thinking about the things you are or could be worrying about. Purge those thoughts from your mind by writing them down. This is like making a deal with your unconscious mind that you will worry about the items on the list, but not right now. Once you have the list, your mind can focus on more immediate and important tasks.

At the end of the day or in a convenient moment, return to the Worry About It Later list. You will probably find that many of the things have gone away or already satisfactorily resolved themselves. It will feel good to cross those things off the list and will make you more aware of the areas where you worry and just how unnecessary it can be.

Your mind will wander, and when you realise that you are thinking about anything other than the Worry About It Later list, return your focus to the writing meditation. Continue until the timer goes off.

- - -

Journal

Type: Plans and Getting Things Done
Summary: Write a simple daily journal with at least one goal, and later reflect on progress
Time: 2–10 minutes

This is a great technique for starting a journal or journaling habit.

Set a timer for 2–10 minutes. At the top of the page write the date or "Journal", and then proceed to write one goal for the day, some steps to complete the goal plus any other thoughts. Reflect on this goal's status at the end of the day.

Choose one goal for the day (or no more than three goals). Also write any steps you will need to take to complete that goal. At the end of the day, on the same page, write whether the goal was completed and any reflections about why, why not or how you could have improved. You might also write one thing you are grateful for or an affirmation or meaningful quote. Try it for a week or for a month. Do it every day and make an effort to establish the habit.

UJ Ramdas and Alex Ikonn created a kind of goal journal in 2013 called "The 5-Minute Journal" that uses a daily affirmation, a weekly challenge, gratitude writing and the question "what would make today great?" This kind of daily writing exercise will help you focus on short term goals, complete tasks and induce positive change.

Your mind will wander, and when you realise that you are thinking about anything other than the daily journal entry, return your focus to the writing meditation. Continue until the timer goes off.

- - -

Last Year Next Year

Type: Plans and Getting Things Done
Summary: Reflect on your life 12 months ago and 12 months from now
Time: 10–20 minutes

This is a good meditation for reflecting on how your life has changed in the last year, and where you hope to be 12 months from now.

Set a timer for 10–20 minutes. At the top of the page write "Last Year Next Year", and then proceed to reflect on your life 12 months ago and goals for 12 months from now.

First, write a long list or many paragraphs about your life 12 months ago, focusing on the things that have changed or that you have achieved during the last year. For instance:

- family and relationships
- big life changes and new responsibilities
- worries or concerns that have resolved themselves
- how your career, job or financial situation has changed
- things acquired
- the most meaningful events or actions or decisions during the last year.

Next, write a long list or many paragraphs about your life 12 months from now, focusing on goals or changes that you would like to make. For instance:

- how to bring more meaning to your life during the next year
- improvements to family or other important relationships
- your desired financial situation
- something you would like to buy or acquire
- thoughts about your job, career and work colleagues
- trips, vacations, holidays to take.

This meditation may lead to important insights about how you change (or not) in the short term, how important things become unimportant and vice versa. This is a great way to reflect on the path of your life and the actions you need to take to use your time wisely and bring more meaning to your life.

Your mind will wander, and when you realise that you are thinking about anything other than reflecting on last year or next year, return your focus to the writing meditation. Continue until the timer goes off.

- - -

Elevator Pitch

Type: Plans and Getting Things Done
Summary: Write a short, succinct sales pitch about an idea you have
Time: 5–20 minutes

Set a timer for 5–20 minutes. At the top of the page write a goal, and then proceed to write a proposal to someone who might be able to help with that goal, or someone who is a gatekeeper for moving forward.

Write an elevator pitch – a short, concise sales pitch – to persuade that person to help you in achieving a goal or providing financial assistance for your idea.

A good elevator pitch will be short and succinct and include:

- An explanation about how your idea solves a common problem
- A unique selling point, i.e. what makes this idea special
- Make it personal – why you and why them
- A specific action you want from the person
- What happens next? If they accept, what is the next step that you will take together?

When crafting your elevator pitch you might also think about using an analogy to make it more relatable, or using an open-ended rhetorical question that supports your conclusions.

Keep in mind that you are crafting a speech, which could be written as prose in your spoken voice, or a speech outline in bullet points. An elevator pitch is necessarily short – one or two paragraphs, ten or fewer sentences – and the finished speech will only be about two minutes in duration.

Your mind will wander, and when you realise that you are thinking about anything other than the elevator pitch, return your focus to the writing meditation. Continue until the timer goes off.

- - -

Who, What, How, Why

Type: Plans and Getting Things Done
Summary: Write about who you are, what you do, how you do it and why you do it
Time: 10–20 minutes

This can be an enlightening exercise which is short, difficult and reflective. It is particularly useful when you are at a crossroads or have a difficult decision to make.

Set a timer for 10–20 minutes. At the top of the page write "Who, What, How, Why", then proceed to write about who you are, what you do, how you do it and why you do it.

Divide a page into the following sections:

- Who I Am
- What I Do
- How I Do It
- Why I Do It (and/or Who I Do It For)

With these simple but profound headings, contemplate and write the answers. They are intentionally open ended and you can interpret "who", "what", "how" and "why" however you like. Start with a simple one sentence answer to each question and don't deliberate; just write what comes to mind. After briefly answering the questions, take more time to write a longer response for each. There may be more than one answer to a question, and you can use the writing time to explore multiple answers or different possible answers.

Your mind will wander, and when you realise that you are thinking about anything other than who you are, what you do, how you do it and why you do it, return your focus to the writing meditation. Continue until the timer goes off.

- - -

Goal Step-Plan

Type: Plans and Getting Things Done
Summary: Write a goal and some specific steps for achieving that goal
Time: 5–20 minutes

Set a timer for 5–20 minutes. At the top of the page write a goal, and then proceed to write a number of small chronological steps for achieving that goal.

The big goal that you write at the top of the page could be a goal for this year, a life goal, a career goal or a bucket list item. It could be something private and meaningful, practical or financial. Avoid vague goals like "be happier" or "make more money". Instead it should be a goal that is achievable through specific actions.

Break down this goal into many small steps. Write down things that you can do today, this week and this month towards that goal. Think of milestones along the way and what steps can get you to those intermediate goals. Think of timelines for achieving the smaller milestones on the way to the big goal. Refer back often, and you can even repeat the exercise every day with the daily and weekly goals changing as needed.

Your mind will wander, and when you realise that you are thinking about anything other than the step plan for achieving your goal, return your focus to the writing meditation. Continue until the timer goes off.

- - -

Resignation Letter, plus Suggestions

Type: Plans and Getting Things Done
Summary: Write a resignation letter to your boss, including suggestions for fixing the things that are broken at your place of business
Time: 10–20 minutes

This can be a cathartic exercise when you are frustrated with your job or employer, and also a great way to initiate change.

Set a timer for 10–20 minutes. At the top of the page write "Resignation Letter", and then proceed to write a letter of resignation to your current boss, also including suggestions for improving the organisation and how your replacement could be more effective and successful.

Writing a letter of resignation can be a great exercise to cleanse your mind of all the negative thoughts you have about your job or career, to clarify exactly what you'd like to say to management, and to consider possible areas of influence and improvement. It can be cathartic to write the resignation letter, even if you aren't intending to resign (yet!).

Since you aren't actually going to give this to your boss, write at length what you really feel. Use this as a chance to get things off your chest. At the same time, write constructive feedback about how to improve the organisation, how management can manage better, and suggestions for changes to allow your successor to be better at the job than you feel you have been.

This writing meditation also works well as a journal entry, in the form of ways you can take more ownership of the direction of the organisation or clarify what and how to effect change every day at work.

Your mind will wander, and when you realise that you are thinking about anything other than the resignation letter and ways to improve your organisation, return your focus to the writing meditation. Continue until the timer goes off.

- - -

Who/How Can I Help Today

Type: Plans and Getting Things Done
Summary: Write a list of ten (or more) ideas about people you can help today and how
Time: 5–15 minutes

Aristotle wrote that finding happiness and fulfilment is achieved "by loving rather than in being loved." Psychologist Carol Ryff, on reviewing the writings of numerous philosophers, says that relationships with others are "a central feature of a positive, well-lived life" (Ryff, Singer; JoHS, 2008).

This is a great exercise for planning to be more generous and charitable, as well as to find ways to add more meaning and happiness to your life.

Set a timer for 5–10 minutes. At the top of the page write "Who/How I can Help Today", then proceed to write a list of at least ten ideas of specific people you could help, and how you could help them. These people could be family and friends, neighbours or people who you interact with regularly but don't know directly. It could be people at work, on the street, in a café or restaurant, volunteers, charitable organisations or even communities of people. Likely, you could do many things big and small to have an impact. Use this time to think creatively about who and how you could help.

Stretch your creative muscles and write as many ideas as possible. Like Aristotle said, this could help you find some of your own happiness and fulfilment.

Your mind will wander, and when you realise that you are thinking about anything other than your list of ideas about people you can help today and how, return your focus to the writing meditation. Continue until the timer goes off.

- - -

Predictive Journaling

Type: Plans and Getting Things Done
Summary: Write an end-of-day journal entry in the morning, predicting what will happen today
Time: 10–20 minutes

Set a timer for 10–20 minutes. At the top of the page write the date or "What Happened Today", and then proceed to write an end-of-day journal entry, but do so at the beginning of the day, predicting in advance what will happen throughout the day.

As a morning writing meditation, write a journal entry as if it was the end of the day. Write in the past tense and start at the point of your writing meditation time, then describe how the rest of the day unfolded. What did you do and where did you go? What goals did you complete and how? What thing which you have been procrastinating on did you take the steps to complete? How did you get out of your comfort zone? What was a situation where you made yourself proud? Keep it positive and aspirational.

You'll be surprised how well you can predict the future, and how you can influence your day with this exercise.

Your mind will wander, and when you realise that you are thinking about anything other than the predictive journal entry, return your focus to the writing meditation. Continue until the timer goes off.

- - -

Tips for More Effective Writing Meditations

The following are 15 tips for more effective writing meditations.

1. **Just do it**. Try different writing meditations and enjoy the time spent writing.

2. Don't worry about grammar and spelling; just **get thoughts into words** on a page.

3. Focus on a writing meditation for 5 to 20 minutes. **Set a timer**.

4. **Write a lot quickly.** Write by hand in cursive or short-hand if possible, although typing fast into a word processor can work as well if you avoid editing.

5. Write in an inexpensive, thin notebook that is easy to carry and convenient to **refer back to**, but that you won't mind spilling coffee on or leaving on an airplane.

6. **Don't wait for perfect conditions** or perfect quiet. Work with your environment and try for the best conditions under various circumstances, but be flexible and unfussy.

7. Meditate in **a place where you won't be disturbed** if possible, but you can do it anywhere. It is fine to have a preferred quiet spot or desk, but don't be too tied down to that single spot either. You can write in a park, on a plane, at work, in your bedroom, in a noisy or quiet place, with earbuds, standing, sitting, lying, etc.

8. Do it **any time that's convenient**, although the morning is probably best.

9. **Try new techniques** and find out what is best for you.

10. **Be open**, honest and authentic with the knowledge that no one else is going to read it.

11. Writing meditations are thoughtful and reflective, but you should try to **combine action with reflection.** Your new awareness and creativity should be followed up with daily actions.

12. Reflect on how you can **improve your writing meditations**, or how meditation can improve other aspects of your life.

13. It is not unusual to remember important things or for unrelated **creative insights** to appear during

writing meditation. Avoid the temptation to break concentration on the current writing prompt, but revisit after the writing meditation is complete or the timer goes off.

14. Your **mind will wander** to other thoughts, the past and present and other things you need to do. When you realise you are elsewhere, return to the writing meditation.

15. **It is a practice**. You are practising over months and years. Each time it is a practice. The only way to get better is to practice.

16. Bonus tip: Find time to **meditate** as well. My book "Meditations: 50 meditation techniques" provides simple and clear instructions for 50 different meditation techniques including mantra, mindfulness, breath counting, relaxation, metta, writing, visualisation, body scan and more. Find it at Amazon.

- - -

Questions, comments, ideas? Send me an email: hamilton2075 [at] gmail [dot] com

Very Short Writing Meditations

Suggestions for very short writing meditations when you only have a few minutes to spare

"If my doctor told me I had only six minutes to live, I wouldn't brood. I'd type a little faster."
--Isaac Asimov

Sometimes you only have a few minutes to write, either as soon as you wake up, or in a waiting room, or at your desk between meetings. On the next page are some ideas for using that time effectively.

Type: Various
Summary: Writing meditations which you can do in a very short period of time
Time: 1–5 minutes

Here are a few ideas of meditations which are described elsewhere in this book, but which you can do with limited time:

- List of 10 Bad Ideas
- Worry About It Later
- Purge
- Haiku or Limerick
- Affirmations or Goal Writing
- Pros and Cons
- Gratitude List

Find a place where you are unlikely to be disturbed. Sit in a comfortable position and set a timer for 1–5 minutes. Spend up to a minute settling and preparing, then take a few deep breaths and begin to write.

Proceed with a very short writing meditation, modified from the longer version described in this book if necessary. Continue until the timer goes off, or until you need to focus your attention elsewhere.

- - -

Five More Writing Meditations

If you found the prompts and tips in this book useful, please visit http://bit.ly/writingmed5 for five more writing meditation prompts which are not included in this book. Alternatively, you can email me at the address below and I will send you the PDF of those techniques, which include: Life as a Story Plot, Five Unconscious Thoughts, Scribe Meditation and more.

I would love to hear from you with questions, comments, things forgotten, ideas for new techniques, modifications, suggestions or anything else. Which technique is most effective for you? Send me an email at hamilton2075 [at] gmail [dot] com or connect with me on Facebook.

CM Hamilton, Winter 2018

- - -

Also by the Author: 50 Meditation Techniques

ALSO BY THE AUTHOR. Visit https://bit.ly/50med for an extract from CM Hamilton's book, *"Meditations: 50 Meditation Techniques and 25 Tips for Starting, Improving and Maintaining a Meditation Practice"* © 2018.

There are many ways to meditate, and each person's practice can grow and evolve over time in different situations and at different stages of life. Trying different techniques is an excellent way to experience meditation, as well as to find a meditation practice that is right for you, right now.

"Meditations" by CM Hamilton provides simple and clear instructions for 50 different meditation techniques including mantra, mindfulness, breath counting, relaxation, metta, writing, visualisation, body scan and more. The techniques are divided into three categories: focused attention, monitoring or mindfulness, and intentional thinking. At the end of the book there are 25

tips for starting, improving, and maintaining a meditation practice.

"Meditations: 50 Meditation Techniques and 25 Tips for Starting, Improving and Maintaining a Meditation Practice" is available via Amazon.

For an extract of the book with instructions for six fundamental meditation techniques, visit https://bit.ly/50med.

- - -

Meditations for Sleep

ALSO BY THE AUTHOR. Visit https://bit.ly/sleepmed for an extract from CM Hamilton's book, *"Meditations for Sleep: Overcome Insomnia and Sleep Well"* © 2019.

Do you need relief from insomnia? Do you want a short book with information, suggestions, meditations, tips and techniques for restful sleep?

"Meditations for Sleep" provides an overview of sleep and insomnia, describes some common causes of sleep problems, and includes many suggested solutions. The book also provides simple, clear instructions for 20 meditation techniques including mindfulness, breathing and visualisation techniques.

We all know what sleep is, but that doesn't mean that defining this mysterious part of our lives is simple. The transition from conscious wakefulness to unconscious sleep is nearly instantaneous—you're awake one moment, asleep the next. Unfortunately stress, busy schedules and external factors can make perfect sleep habits difficult or impossible. You can do many things to put yourself in the best position to get restful sleep, and the suggestions and meditation techniques in this book have been effective for me to overcome periods of acute insomnia.

"Meditations for Sleep: Overcome Insomnia and Sleep Well" is available via Amazon.

For an extract of the book with instructions for four sleeping meditations, visit https://bit.ly/sleepmed.

- - -

About the Author

CM Hamilton has been collecting meditation techniques and practising meditation for more than twenty years. Some of his favourite writing meditations include: 10 Bad Ideas, Things-to-do This Weekend and Stream of Consciousness. In regular meditation practice he most often uses some combination of breath counting, mantra and visualisation. The author is uncomfortable in flight turbulence, has studied philosophy and finance, and prefers Islay whisky. He enjoys the French language, German culture, Mexican food, and one time went hang gliding in Switzerland. CM Hamilton has spent most of his life in England and Texas, and currently lives in London with his wife and three kids. He has never been to Copenhagen, and often forgets to smile. Quidquid latine dictum, altum videtur.

email: hamilton2075 [at] gmail [dot] com
facebook: @hamilton2075
amazon: https://amazon.com/author/cmhamilton

Excerpt from "Meditations: 50 Meditation Techniques"

The following pages are an extract from **"Meditations: 50 Meditation Techniques"** by CM Hamilton

Published by CM Hamilton
© 2018 London

The book provides very simple meditation instructions as follows:

Find a place where you are unlikely to be disturbed. Sit in a comfortable position and set a timer for 5-20 minutes. Close your eyes and spend up to a minute settling and relaxing your muscles. Focus your mind on something – breaths, sounds, thoughts, words, bodily sensations (e.g. a technique). Your mind will naturally wander away and you will lose focus. When you realize that your mind has wondered, shift your attention back to your meditation focus. For 5 to 20 minutes you will repeat this process of: focus, loss of focus, return to focus, loss of focus, return to focus.

There are many different meditation techniques and ways to classify them, but for the purposes of the book, they are divided into three main types:

I.   Focused Attention (Concentration) - focus your attention and concentration narrowly and repeatedly on one item. Fifteen techniques are included in the book.

II.   Monitoring (Mindfulness) - monitor a sensation or experience in the present moment. Sixteen techniques are included in the book.

III.   Intentional Thinking - focus attention on an intentional thought process or visualisation. Twenty techniques are included in the book.

Two of the techniques that are included in the book, Breath Counting and Body Scan, are presented here:

Breath Counting

Type: Focused Attention (Concentration)
Summary: Concentrate on counting breath cycles up to 4 or 10
Time: 1-20 minutes

Find a place where you are unlikely to be disturbed. Sit in a comfortable position and set a timer for 1-20 minutes. Close your eyes and spend up to a minute settling and relaxing your muscles.

Breathe naturally in long or short breaths, whatever is comfortable. When settled, begin to count the inhalations from 1-4 and then start again. Count in your mind:

(Inhale) 1 (exhale), (inhale) 2 (exhale), (inhale) 3 (exhale), (inhale) 4 (exhale), (inhale) 1 (exhale), (inhale) 2 (exhale)...

It is more difficult than it seems. Concentrate on the small area between your nostrils and upper lip and notice how the breath feels entering and leaving you while passing over this area. If you lose count, start again at 1. Some may find it easier to think "and" on the exhalation:

(Inhale) 1 (exhale) "and", (inhale) 2 (exhale) "and", (inhale) 3 (exhale) "and", (inhale) 4 (exhale) "and", (inhale) 1 (exhale) "and", (inhale) 2 (exhale) "and"...

...or some may find it easier to say the number on both inhalation and the exhalation:

(Inhale) 1 (exhale) 1, (inhale) 2 (exhale) 2, (inhale) 3 (exhale) 3, (inhale) 4 (exhale) 4, (inhale) 1 (exhale) 1, (inhale) 2 (exhale) 2...

You can count to 4 or any other number. However, for many people it is common to lose count or accidentally continue counting past 10, so a smaller number is better.

Your mind will wander, and when you realise that you are thinking about anything other than your breathing, return your focus to counting breaths and how they feel on the small area between your nostrils and upper lip. Continue until the timer goes off.

Body Scan

Type: Monitoring (Mindfulness)
Summary: Consecutively monitor parts of your body, sensations and your surroundings in a deliberate way
Time: 5-20 minutes

Regularly practicing a body scan can help you enhance your ability to bring your full attention to real-time experiences happening in the present moment, which is helpful when emotions or thoughts feel uncontrollable. It also helps you to understand how the body and mind, pain and no pain, exist within the same body.

Find a place where you are unlikely to be disturbed. Sit or lie in a comfortable position and set a timer for 5-20 minutes. Close your eyes and spend up to a minute settling and relaxing your muscles.

Notice the areas where your body makes contact with the seat or floor or bed, wherever you happen to be. Bring awareness to your body while breathing in and out. When you're ready, intentionally breathe in, and move your attention to your head. Notice everything you can about this area of your body – temperature, pains, sensations, feelings, weight, posture, muscles, curves, aches, skin, pulse, joints, bones, sounds, tingling, pressure, tightness, temperature, soreness, or anything else. Spend some time noticing everything you can, and when you think you have noticed everything, spend a little more time.

When the time feels right, move on to the next part of the body. You might choose to do a systematic body scan from top to bottom, or start at the feet and work up, or move about randomly. The main point is being curious, aware and open to what you are noticing. Investigate the sensations as fully as possible, and then intentionally release the focus of attention before shifting to the next area to explore.

Your mind will wander, but keep coming back to your body and start again where you left off or proceed to a new part of the body. Continue until the timer goes off.

- - -

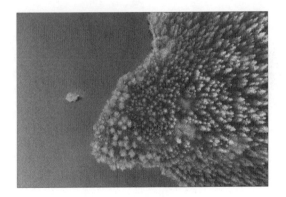

thank you

CM Hamilton
hamilton2075 [at] gmail [dot] com

38133249R00061

Made in the USA
Middletown, DE
05 March 2019